ASPECTS OF BRITISH HISTORY BEYOND 1066

THE BUILDING OF BRITAIN'S RAILWAYS

Catherine Chambers

Raintree is an imprint of Capstone Global Library Limited, a company incorporated in England and Wales having its registered office at 264 Banbury Road, Oxford, OX2 7DY – Registered company number: 6695582

www.raintree.co.uk

myorders@raintree.co.uk

Edited by Helen Cox Cannons
Designed by Steve Mead
Original illustrations © Capstone Global Library Limited 2017
Picture research by Ruth Smith
Production by Victoria Fitzgerald
Originated by Capstone Global Library Limited
Printed and bound in India

ISBN 978 1 4747 3420 2 (hardback)
20 19 18 17 16
10 9 8 7 6 5 4 3 2 1

ISBN 978 1 4747 3423 3 (paperback)
21 20 19 18 17
10 9 8 7 6 5 4 3 2 1

British Library Cataloguing in Publication Data
A full catalogue record for this book is available from the British Library.

Acknowledgements
We would like to thank the following for permission to reproduce photographs: Alamy: David Lyons, 6, DB Pictures, 18, The Keasbury-Gordon Photograph Archive, 17; Capstone Press: 27; Getty Images: Archive Photos, 15, Fox Photos, 21, Hans Wild/The LIFE Picture Collection, 23, Hulton Archive, 7, Robert Sennecke/ullstein bild, 24, Science & Society Picture Library, 9, 10, 13, Steve Winter/National Geographic, 14, The Print Collector, 19, Universal History Archive/UIG, 8; Glow Images: Heritage Images, 29; Granger, NYC - All rights reserved, 20; iStockphoto: BernardAllum, 5; Shutterstock: Andreas Berheide, cover, back cover, HodagMedia, cover, BasPhoto, 12, Everett Historical, 22, i4lcocl2, cover, 25, javarman, background design element, LenaTru, background design element, Meoita, 11, Nick Fox, 4, Nicku, 28t, Peter R Foster IDMA, 26, photocell, back cover, 16, PRILL, background design element, Rob Hyrons, cover; Thinkstock: Photos.com, 28b.

We would like to thank Dr Linsey Hunter at the University of the Highlands and Islands for his invaluable help in the preparation of this book.

CONTENTS

THE BIRTH OF THE STEAM TRAIN 4

TIME FOR THE STEAM LOCOMOTIVE 8

THE GREAT WESTERN RAILWAY 12

RAILWAYS ROCK THE WORLD 14

NO TRAINS WITHOUT TRACKS 16

IT'S ELECTRIFYING! 18

RAILWAY TRAVEL BECOMES POPULAR 20

PULLING TOGETHER 22

BRITISH RAILWAYS 24

THE OLD AND THE NEW 26

TIMELINE 27

RAILWAY BIOGRAPHIES 28

GLOSSARY 30

FIND OUT MORE 31

INDEX 32

THE BIRTH OF THE STEAM TRAIN

Over 200 years ago in Britain, a steam engine was attached to wheels and set upon a flat track. The wheels turned, the machine moved and the first locomotive was born. A new, exciting **transport** revolution called the railway had begun.

THE TROUBLE WITH TRANSPORT

From the 1750s onwards, the new steam engine powered machinery in factories. Faster than ever before, the factories manufactured more and more goods. This period in history is known as the Industrial Revolution. Goods, such as cotton and wool **textiles**, were sold all over the world. So a transport system was needed to cope with this.

A steam train travelling on the Glenfinnan viaduct in the Scottish Highlands in 2015.

COAL, IRON AND WATER — THE THREE TREASURES

Thousands of **barges** carried goods up and down the country in fast-developing canal networks. Canals were straight, **artificial** waterways. They were built to create direct routes between mines and factories, towns and cities. But barges were pulled by horses and were very slow. Carrying goods by horse-drawn cart was no better.

Britain had plenty of coal, iron and water. Together, these things could make and drive factory machinery. Together, they could make steam trains – but they, too, needed to be transported.

This illustration shows a barge going along the Regent's Canal in London in 1828.

HOW DOES A STEAM ENGINE WORK?

Steam engines work by lighting coal under a tank of water. When the water boils, this produces steam that **expands** at high speeds. The steam shoots through tubes and pushes **pistons.** The pistons then help to move the wheels.

NO TRAIN WITHOUT TRACKS

In the early 1600s, businessman Huntingdon Beaumont (1560–1624) had an idea to lay wooden tracks for wagons to run from coal mines to the coast. His revolutionary wagon wheel had a flange, or rim, that clutched the track securely. It was a big hit. From this time, tracks improved and changed from wood to iron. But horse-drawn wagons that ran along them were slow.

MAKING TRAIN HISTORY

Richard Trevithick (1771–1833) was a Cornishman who had a big idea. He believed that a steam-powered engine could roll along existing tracks that served local iron works in Wales. An engine that moved smoothly and at a constant speed would be faster and safer than a horse-drawn wagon. His big idea became the first locomotive: the Penydarren Tramroad engine.

On its first run, the engine's chimney hit a low bridge. Both the chimney and the bridge were damaged.

HORSEPOWER

From 1807, Oystermouth Railway became the world's first public railway that was not owned by a mining company. It took passengers from Swansea to Oystermouth in Wales. The first carriages were horse-drawn, pulled on an existing track called a tramline. Today, engine power is still measured in units of horsepower.

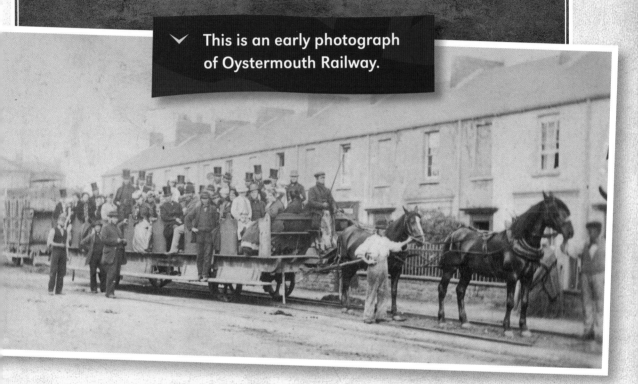

⌄ This is an early photograph of Oystermouth Railway.

PENYDARREN TRAMROAD ENGINE

On 21 February 1804, Trevithick's groundbreaking, 10-ton engine pulled itself nearly 10 miles (16 kilometres), from Merthyr to Abercynon. It reached a speed of five miles (8 kilometres) per hour. The engine could not make the return journey, as it was too heavy for the track. But the outward journey was a triumph and won Trevithick a 500-guinea bet. Today, that sum of money would be worth £50,000!

TIME FOR THE STEAM LOCOMOTIVE

In 1812, the owners of Middleton Colliery in Yorkshire were desperate. There was a shortage of horses to pull their coal wagons along the tracks to the nearby city of Leeds. The British Army needed all the horses for their **cavalry**, to fight in a war with the French. So Middleton Colliery decided to **invest** in the newest idea: the steam engine.

THE EXCITEMENT OF *SALAMANCA*

Colliery supervisor John Blenkinsop (1783–1831) and engineer Matthew Murray (1765–1826) developed the *Salamanca* locomotive. Blenkinsop solved the problem of heavy engines slipping. He attached extra-cogged wheels on each side of the engine. These wheels fitted into a grooved track, gripping it firmly.

> A steam engine could pull a load up to 50 times heavier than a horse.

A RIVAL ENGINE — *PUFFING BILLY*

Soon after, in Wylam Colliery, Durham, William Hedley (1779–1843) developed the *Puffing Billy* locomotive. One new design feature was its two **cylinders** attached to the sides of the boiler, which were kept hot with steam jackets. *Puffing Billy* worked for 48 years and can now be seen in London's Science Museum.

TRACK FACTS

The word *locomotive* was first used to describe a moving, steam-powered coal train. This shows the importance of the steam train's first role, which was to haul coal. The steam engine itself was powered first by **coke**, which is the purest and most **efficient** form of coal.

This is an early photograph of *Puffing Billy*.

STEPHENSONS STEAM AHEAD!

The *Salamanca* and *Puffing Billy* excited businessmen. A powerful steam engine could pull more goods and passengers, and faster, than horses or canal **barges**. Among many upcoming railway engineers, self-taught George Stephenson (1781–1848) stood out. In 1825, the family business, Robert Stephenson & Co., was paid £1,200 for two engines to roll on the Stockton and Darlington Railway. This was the first public railway to use steam engines.

TRACK FACTS

The Stephensons' Stockton and Darlington locomotives pulled 36 wagons across 9 miles (14 kilometres) of track in just 2 hours. They achieved these speeds by squeezing the steam at the base of the chimney and shooting it through 25 tubes instead of a single or double one.

∧ One hundred years after its opening, in 1925, crowds gathered to celebrate the Stockton & Darlington Railway line.

THE *ROCKET* BURSTS ONTO THE SCENE

George Stephenson was also famous for laying tracks, especially the new Liverpool to Manchester line. But he and his son Robert (1803–1859) had to compete with other engineers to build the engines for it. So at the 1829 Rainhill Trials near Liverpool, they entered the *Rocket*. It won with a record speed of 36 miles (58 kilometres) per hour. The *Rocket* became famous.

⟨ Stephenson's *Rocket*

For more about Robert and George Stephenson, turn to page 28

INVICTA

Robert Stephenson's locomotive *Invicta* sparked a new idea: the commuter train. Commuter trains would **transport** workers quickly from a town or village to a city, where there were many jobs. *Invicta* ran along a 6-mile (9.5-kilometre) line that linked the small seaside town of Whitstable to the city of Canterbury in south-east England.

THE GREAT WESTERN RAILWAY

In 1832, a group of **investors** raised money for the longest rail service at that time. It was named The Great Western Railway. It was completed in 1841 and ran from London to the thriving port of Bristol in the west. This was a distance of 106 miles (170 kilometres). The Great Western Railway increased the fame of its chief engineer, Isambard Kingdom Brunel (1806–1859).

For more about Isambard Kingdom Brunel, turn to page 29

↑ The Great Western Railway stopped at London's grand Paddington Station. This was also designed by Brunel.

A FASTER TRACK

Brunel's great engineering triumph was changing the width, or **gauge**, of the track. He worked out that a 7-foot (2-metre) track width enabled the engine to go faster. Brunel went on to design 1,000 miles (1,600 kilometres) of track in Britain and Ireland, as well as many bridges and tunnels.

CONQUERING HILLS AND VALLEYS

Hills were difficult obstacles to Britain's railway engineers. In 1793, Derbyshire's new Fritchley Tunnel proved successful for Benjamin Outram (1764–1805). Outram's great idea allowed a horse-drawn railway to tunnel through from his Critch limestone quarries to Crompton Canal. He firmly believed in the idea of a seamless network of rail tracks that could unite the country.

Steep valleys were also difficult to overcome. Strong cast-iron bridges were designed to support heavy loads on tracks. One of the first of these was Crawshaw Woods Bridge, along the Leeds & Selby Railway. James Walker (1781–1862) designed it in 1830.

THE LIVES OF NAVVIES

Navvies were the men and women who shifted great heaps of earth to build Britain's railways. By 1850, about 250,000 navvies were building tracks, often in harsh conditions.

RAILWAYS ROCK THE WORLD

From the 1840s, Britain's rail **investors** and engineers hurried to find success across the globe. They were encouraged by Queen Victoria's government to build tracks throughout the **British Empire**, from Australia to Africa to Canada. Trains provided fast **transport** for valuable **raw materials**.

CROSSING INDIA

India was a British **colony** during the 1800s. In 1853, an engine pulled out of Bombay (now Mumbai), holding 14 carriages packed with 400 passengers. A 21-gun salute and cheering crowds celebrated. By 1880, the Indian Railway's tracks covered 9,000 miles (14,500 kilometres). They crossed very challenging mountainous **terrain**.

⌄ The *Himalayan Bird* steam train still travels through the hills of Darjeeling, India.

OPENING UP AMERICA

The United States's vast lands range from deserts to mountain ranges and swamps to raging rivers. How could tracks be laid across them? The east–west journey from the Atlantic to Pacific Ocean coasts was the biggest challenge of all. On 10 May 1869, the Pacific Railroad was completed. It was nearly 2,000 miles (3,220 kilometres) long. The need for the journey to be made by horse-drawn wagon was coming to an end.

TRACK FACTS

In 1869, US engineer George Westinghouse invented the first automatic air brake. This new braking system made brakes work better and meant safer travel. It also meant that Britain was no longer leading the world in rail technology.

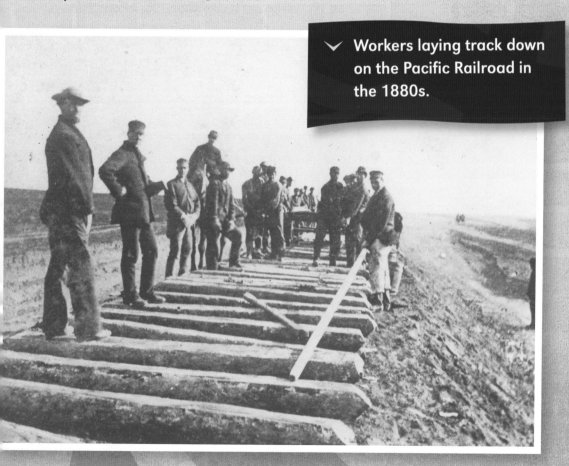

Workers laying track down on the Pacific Railroad in the 1880s.

NO TRAINS WITHOUT TRACKS

Tracks for wheeled vehicles were invented over 4,000 years ago in Sumeria, in the Middle East. But by the 1800s, the burden on tracks was much greater. Heavy locomotives pulled wagons full of coal and iron. The weight of these gave track engineers a huge challenge.

STEADY AND STURDY

Tracks were set on a camber (slightly domed ground), allowing rainwater to drain down the sides. A layer of sand covered it, topped with a **ballast** of thick stones. Then, long wooden **sleepers**, or ties, were laid down like a ladder. They kept the steel tracks laid on top of them at equal distances. Railway tracks were made to a certain width, or **gauge**, to carry the trains within each region.

Sleepers were usually made of hard or soft wood. Today, many are made of concrete.

SAFETY AND SIGNALS

In 1830, a railway **investor**, William Huskisson (1770–1830), was hit by a passing train on the Liverpool line. At the time, signals were just flags waved at ground level. After this, manned stop–go signals from signal boxes came into use at busier junctions and tracks. In 1902, improved electricity supplies led to the first automatic signal between Andover and Grateley in southern England.

⌄ This is an early photograph of a signal box, taken in Victorian times.

PADIHAM STATION WEST

TRACK FACTS

How did engines turn around? In 1839, four rail companies in Derby City wanted an engine-driven, 12-metre (39-feet) turntable. It was designed by Robert Stephenson. You can still visit the Derby Roundhouse and turntable today.

TOO MANY RAILWAY COMPANIES

By 1914, there were about 20,000 miles (32,000 kilometres) of track run by 120 companies in Britain. But there were no safety rules between the companies. In 1923, the British government decided to group all the railway companies into four regional companies. This improved rail safety management.

IT'S ELECTRIFYING!

Steam locomotives needed constant **refuelling** with coal and water. Their chimneys churned out dangerous fumes that turned the skies yellow. It was time to use an easier, cleaner power source: electricity.

SEASIDE TRACKS

On 3 August 1883, inventor and engineer Magnus Volk (1851–1937) launched the first electric train service in Brighton. The train ran for a quarter of a mile (half a kilometre) along the seafront.

Volk's electric train service still runs along the Brighton seafront today.

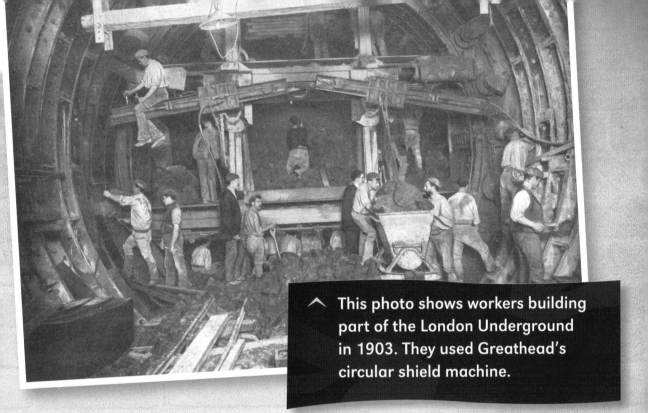

GOING UNDERGROUND

The increasing use of electricity in train engineering sparked the development of the London Underground. In 1843, the new Thames Tunnel that ran under the River Thames inspired a London solicitor, Charles Pearson. Pearson suggested using tunnels to create an underground railway. Finally, in 1863, the first Metropolitan Railway tunnel was opened.

The first tunnels were just deep trenches lined with brick walls and covered with a brick dome. But in 1866, the City and Southern Subway Company ploughed a "tube" line with a new, circular shield machine invented by J. H. Greathead (1844–1896).

The first underground engines were **coke**-fired, like mainline trains. The smoke and fumes that this produced did not stop 9.5 million passengers using underground trains during the first year alone.

RAILWAY TRAVEL BECOMES POPULAR

The first railway carriages of the mid-1800s were open wagons with hard seats. As train travel became popular, they became carriages of comfort, but not for everyone. British society was divided into classes, even on the railways.

COACHES, CARRIAGES AND COMFORT

First-Class carriages were more expensive and comfortable than Second-Class ones. Rich people were provided with foot warmers in chilly weather. In the First-Class dining car, waiters laid silver cutlery and fine china. Stewards served customers travelling in the overnight sleeping carriages. Poor Third-Class ticket-holders still sat on hard wooden seats – if there were seats at all.

Third-Class travel was far from comfortable, as this illustration from 1847 shows!

THE ORIENT EXPRESS

From 1919–1977 the glamorous *Orient Express* was the height of luxury. It took passengers from Paris to the Turkish city of Constantinople, now Istanbul. In 1982, it began running again between London and Venice.

DREAM TRAIN — THE *FLYING SCOTSMAN*

Every railwayman wanted to serve on the fast, smart *Flying Scotsman*. It was named the *Flying Scotsman* as it reduced the London to Edinburgh journey to just eight hours. It was built in 1924 for the London and North Eastern Railway. Its stewards served parties of wealthy tourists and businessmen travelling between the two cities.

This is the *Flying Scotsman* in 1928, when it was quite new.

PULLING TOGETHER

During World War I (1914–1918), railways **transported** soldiers, horses and heavy military weapons for the first time. Trains were used in all of the warring countries. In Britain, 100,000 railway workers left the railways to fight in the war. For the first time, women took their place.

This photo of a special carriage in an ambulance train shows wounded soldiers in their beds.

CARRIAGES FOR CARING

Many carriages were fitted out as sleepers to carry troops travelling hundreds of miles to war. Special carriages were made for the thousands of wounded servicemen and women. These ambulance trains were almost one-third of a mile (0.5 kilometres) long. They transported patients to hospitals all over Europe. Carriages were like proper hospital wards, and medical staff lived on board.

TARGETING TRAINS IN WORLD WAR II

During World War II (1939–1945), the British government took control of the railway companies to **coordinate** the movement of troops and supplies. At night, railway stations in Britain were totally blacked out. This helped confuse German bomber planes targeting stations and tracks.

TRACK FACTS

By 1916, only 10,000 tons of British supplies were reaching France on its rail network each week. Britain and the United States then provided 2,000 miles (3,219 kilometres) of extra track. By 1917, 200,000 tons of supplies were reaching the battlefields.

By 1940, most of Europe was in the hands of **Nazi** Germany. British and Allied undercover agents tried to stop their movements by blowing up railway bridges and junctions.

ESCAPE TO THE COUNTRY

Just before World War II, the British government was afraid of bombs falling on cities. So 3 million people were evacuated to safety. Many of them were children. Most people were transported by train from cities to the countryside during the first four days of September 1939.

BRITISH RAILWAYS

In 1947, all British railway businesses came under total government control. In business this is known as nationalization. The national rail network was named British Railways the following year.

THE END OF STEAM

British Railways made great changes to trains and tracks. They reduced **pollution**, noise and the need for a huge workforce. By the 1950s, **diesel** engines were replacing steam locomotives.

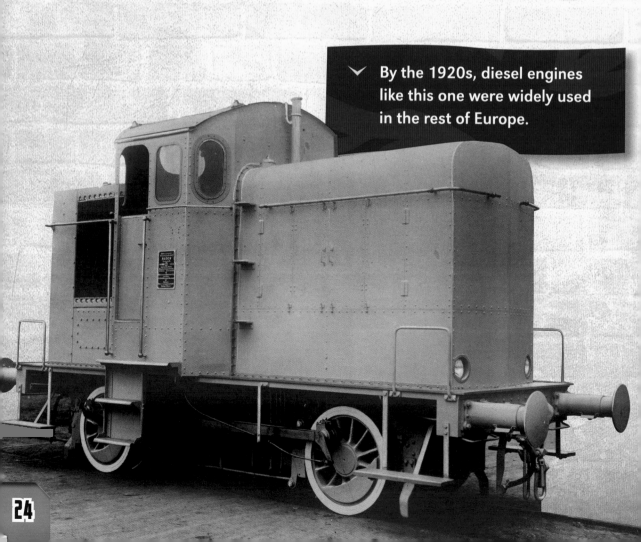

By the 1920s, diesel engines like this one were widely used in the rest of Europe.

ELECTRIC TRACKS AND AUTOMATION

By the 1960s, trains that ran on **electrified** tracks finally put an end to the steam engine. Automatic signalling was introduced. Computerized **freight**-monitoring systems kept track of over 200,000 freight trains at once. New seamless, welded tracks made trains run smoothly and much more quietly. The clickety-clack of the steam engine was a thing of the past.

⌃ Electric cables that ran both overhead and along the ground changed the look of railway tracks.

BEECHING'S BOMBSHELL

British Railways could not make a **profit**, in spite of all the changes they made. So in 1963, the Minister of Transport Dr Richard Beeching (1913–1985), suggested making heavy cuts to train services. Small branch lines were closed and their stations abandoned. The favourite *Flying Scotsman* was retired. People were furious.

TRACK FACTS

Between 1961 and 1969, 6,116 miles (9,843 kilometres) of British Railways track was ripped up and 4,023 stations were closed.

THE OLD AND THE NEW

Britain is still a train-loving nation and continues to build its railways. The Channel Tunnel that runs between England and France opened in May 1994. On 14 November 2007, High Speed 1 (HS1) trains began to speed through there. They flew along at 186 miles (300 kilometres) per hour, travelling from London to Paris in just 2 hours 15 minutes.

STEAM RISES AGAIN

Amateur steam train enthusiasts began to **refurbish** old locomotives. They opened old lines and stations. Now, more than 100 **heritage** railways with over 700 working engines are run and maintained by 23,000 volunteers. Some tracks closed under Dr Beeching will soon be opened up to modern trains.

WHAT HAPPENED TO THE *FLYING SCOTSMAN?*

From 1963, the famous *Flying Scotsman* toured the UK, the United States and Australia. It was bought and sold several times and needed a lot of repair. In 2016, it toured round stations in Britain and is now cared for by the National Railway Museum.

^ The *Flying Scotsman* was greeted in stations by adoring fans.

TIMELINE

1804
Richard Trevithick builds the first locomotive, named the Penydarren Tramroad engine

1813
John Blenkinsop and Matthew Murray build the *Salamanca*. William Hedley builds *Puffing Billy*.

1825
Robert Stephenson & Co. supplies two engines to roll on the first public track, the Stockton and Darlington Railway

1866
The London underground is built using a new, circular shield machine invented by J. H. Greathead

1832
Isambard Kingdom Brunel engineers the first public passenger and goods line, the Great Western Railway

1829
George and Robert Stephenson design the *Rocket*

1869
the United ates, the First anscontinental ailroad is ompleted

1913
The first **diesel** train operates in Sweden

1914-1918
Trains allow mass **transportation** to battlefields during World War I. Hospital trains are made for the wounded.

1924
The *Flying Scotsman* is built for the London and North Eastern Railway

1950-1960s
The British government closes down thousands of stations and rips up tracks

1950-1960s
Diesel and electric trains take over from steam trains

1947-1948
The British government takes over the railway network and names it British Railways

2007
High Speed 1 (HS1) Eurostar service from London to Paris, Brussels and Lille opens. It travels through the Channel Tunnel.

2016
The *Flying Scotsman* is done up and given to the National Railway Museum

RAILWAY BIOGRAPHIES

GEORGE STEPHENSON (1781–1848)

George Stephenson was born in the north of England, near Newcastle upon Tyne. His father worked on early steam engines used in coal mines. Young George took a keen interest in them. He taught himself to read and write to help him become an engineer.

In 1814, George built his first steam locomotive, the *Blucher*. It hauled coal from Newcastle's Killingworth Colliery. After this, George became famous for designing the *Rocket* locomotive and the Stockton and Darlington railway line. He engineered railways in Belgium and Spain, too.

ROBERT STEPHENSON (1803–1859)

Robert attended Bruce Academy in Newcastle, before working with his father. In 1838, Robert engineered the London & Birmingham Railway. It was the first railway line into London. Robert became famous for designing bridges using metal tubes. One of these was the Victoria Bridge over the St Lawrence River in Canada. He received honours in many countries.

ISAMBARD KINGDOM BRUNEL (1806–1859)

Isambard Kingdom Brunel was born in Portsmouth, on the south coast of England. He was the son of engineer Sir Marc Isambard Brunel. Isambard helped his father build the Thames Tunnel until 1828. An accident stopped Isambard's work there and he struggled with his health for a few years. After returning to work, Isambard designed many bridges and docks. In 1833, he was appointed chief engineer for the Great Western Railway. He advised on railways even as far away as Australia.

ISAMBARD'S WALKING STICK

Isambard owned a walking stick that opened out to 7 feet (just over 2 metres). This was the exact width of the broad **gauge** track. It is said that he used his stick to check that the track was the correct width.

GLOSSARY

artificial made by humans and not by nature

ballast heavy material that adds weight to an object

barge large, flat ship used to transport goods

British Empire territories that were under leadership or control of the British Crown

cavalry unit of soldiers who fight on horseback

coke powdery form of coal used to extract metals from their ores

colony country or area taken over and ruled by another country

coordinate organize activities or people so they work well together

cylinder hollow area inside an engine in which fuel burns to create power

diesel heavy fuel that is burned to make power

efficient working very well and not wasting energy

electrified powered using electricity

expand grow larger

freight goods or cargo

gauge instrument used to measure something

heritage history and traditions handed down from the past

investor someone who provides money for a project in return for a share in the profits

Nazi member of a political party led by Adolf Hitler; the Nazis ruled over Germany from 1933 to 1945

piston small tube that moves up and down inside a larger tube to help power machinery

pollution introduction into the environment of poisonous or harmful substances

profit money that a business makes after expenses have been taken out

raw materials material or substance that is treated or processed and made into a useful finished product

refuel supply or take on more fuel

refurbish repair and make improvements to something

sleeper block of wood that is laid across railway tracks to keep them in place

terrain surface of the land and its physical features

textile woven or knitted fabric or cloth

transport move or carry something or someone from one place to another

FIND OUT MORE

BOOKS

Brunel the Great Engineer, Sally Hewitt (Hachette Books, 2012)

Trains (Exploring Science), Michael Harris and Steve Parker (Armadillo Books, 2016)

Transport: From Walking to High Speed Rail (Timeline History), Elizabeth Raum (Heinemann Library, 2010)

WEBSITES

http://www.bbc.co.uk/education/clips/z9fvr82

This clip shows working steam trains and charts their history.

http://www.bbc.co.uk/schools/primaryhistory/famouspeople/george_stephenson/

There are plenty of facts about George Stephenson and his work on this BBC website.

http://www.bbc.co.uk/schools/primaryhistory/famouspeople/isambard_kingdom_brunel/

You can read lots of information about Isambard Kingdom Brunel here.

INDEX

ambulance trains 22

Beaumont, Huntingdon 6
Beeching, Dr Richard 25, 26
Blenkinsop, John 8, 27
braking systems 15
bridges and viaducts 4, 13, 23, 28, 29
British Railways 24–25
Brunel, Isambard Kingdom 12, 13, 27, 29

canals 5
carriages 7, 20, 22
commuter trains 11

diesel engines 24, 27

electric trains and tracks 18–19, 25, 27
Eurostar 26, 27

Flying Scotsman 21, 25, 26, 27
freight trains 25

gauge 13, 16, 29
Great Western Railway 12–13, 27, 29

Hedley, William 9, 27
heritage railways 26
horsepower 5, 7, 8, 10, 13, 15
Huskisson, William 17

India 14
Industrial Revolution 4
Invicta 11

locomotive, first 4, 27

Murray, Matthew 8, 27

nationalization 24
navvies 13

Orient Express 21
Outram, Benjamin 13
Oystermouth Railway 7

Pacific Railroad 15
Penydarren Tramroad engine 6, 7, 27
public railway, first 7
Puffing Billy 9, 10, 27

Rainhill Trials 11
Rocket 11, 27, 28

Salamanca 8, 10, 27
signals 17, 25
steam engines 4, 5, 6, 8, 9, 10
Stephenson, George 10, 11, 27, 28
Stephenson, Robert 10, 11, 17, 27, 28
Stockton and Darlington Railway 10, 27, 28

tracks 11, 13, 16–17, 23, 25, 29
tramlines 7
Trevithick, Richard 6, 7, 27
tunnels 13, 19, 26, 29
turntables 17

underground railways 19, 27
United States 15, 23, 26, 27

Volk, Magnus 18

Walker, James 13
wartime 22–23, 27
Westinghouse, George 15